LEOPARDS

Jen Green

Grolier
an imprint of

📖SCHOLASTIC

www.scholastic.com/librarypublishing

Published 2009 by Grolier
An imprint of Scholastic Library Publishing
Old Sherman Turnpike, Danbury,
Connecticut 06816

For The Brown Reference Group plc
Project Editor: Jolyon Goddard
Picture Researcher: Clare Newman
Designers: Dave Allen, Jeni Child, John
Dinsdale, Lynne Ross, Sarah Williams
Managing Editors: Bridget Giles, Tim Harris

Volume ISBN-13: 978-0-7172-8027-8
Volume ISBN-10: 0-7172-8027-6

**Library of Congress
Cataloging-in-Publication Data**

Nature's children. Set 4.
   p. cm.
   Includes bibliographical references and
index.
   ISBN 13: 978-0-7172-8083-4
   ISBN 10: 0-7172-8083-7 ((set 4) : alk. paper)
   1. Animals--Encyclopedias, Juvenile. I.
Grolier (Firm)
   QL49.N385 2009
   590.3--dc22
                        2007046315

Printed and bound in China

PICTURE CREDITS

Front Cover: **Nature PL**: Anup Shah.

Back Cover: **Nature PL**: Richard Du Toit;
Shutterstock: EcoPrint, Keith Levit, Stuart
Taylor.

Nature PL: Peter Blackwell 21, Tom
Mangelsen 33, Anup Shah 41, 42, 46, Lynn M.
Stone 17; **Shutterstock**: Richard Costin 34,
EcoPrint 10, Keith Levit 4, 9, 18, 26–27,
Anthony Mahadevan 2–3, 14, Stephen Meese
6, Jakob Metzger 30, Kristian Sekulic 5, 13,
29, 37, Johan Swanepoel 22; **Still Pictures**:
M. Carniel/4nature/Wildlife 45, Martin
Harvey 38.

Contents

Fact File: Leopards 4

The World of Cats 7

Leopard Country 8

Packed with Muscle 11

Spotted Coat 12

In Disguise 15

Black Panthers 16

Long, Swishy Tail 19

Champion Athlete 20

Super Senses 23

What's for Dinner? 24

Claws and Jaws 25

Feature Photo 26–27

Gone Hunting 28

Save It for Later 31

Trespassers Beware! 32

Dotty Ears 35

Leopard Noises 36

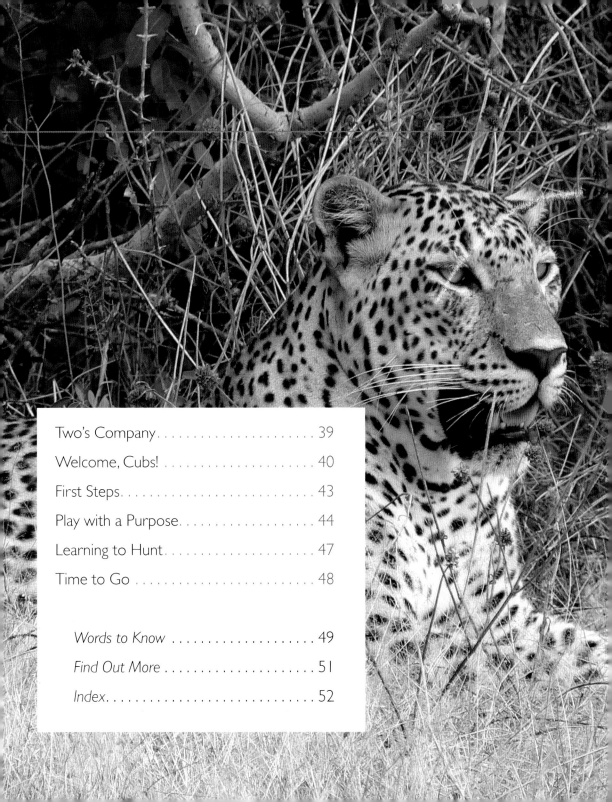

Two's Company. 39

Welcome, Cubs! 40

First Steps. 43

Play with a Purpose. 44

Learning to Hunt. 47

Time to Go 48

Words to Know 49

Find Out More 51

Index. 52

FACT FILE: Leopards

Class	Mammals (Mammalia)
Order	Carnivores (Carnivora)
Family	Cats (Felidae)
Genus	Lions, tigers, jaguars, and leopards (*Panthera*)
Species	Leopard (*Panthera pardus*)
World distribution	Africa, mostly south of the Sahara; western Asia, southern Asia, and Southeast Asia
Habitat	Varied, including forests, grasslands, mountains, and semideserts
Distinctive physical characteristics	Big cats; most leopards have black spots arranged in roselike patterns on a tan background, and a long, thick tail
Habits	Mostly solitary; hunt mainly at night
Diet	Herd animals such as gazelles, zebras, and wildebeest; also pigs, monkeys, birds, fish, and smaller animals; occasionally plants

Introduction

Through the ages, people have admired leopards for their strength, grace, and beautiful spotted coat. Like all members of the cat family, leopards are expert hunters and killers.

Leopards are shy animals that avoid people. For this reason, until recently people knew very little about leopards. However, modern technology, such as hidden cameras and tracking devices, have helped scientists discover more about these fascinating big cats.

The leopard is the least endangered of the big cats.

The snow leopard,
or ounce, lives in the
mountains of central
and southern Asia.

6

The World of Cats

Leopards are cats—and, therefore, relatives of pet cats. Zoologists, or scientists who study animals, divide the cat family into two groups: big cats and small cats. Leopards belong to the big-cat club, along with lions, tigers, and jaguars. The leopard looks very similar to the jaguar, but the two animals live in different parts of the world. Other big cats include the clouded leopard and the snow leopard. They are related to the leopard, like other cats, but there is only one species of true leopard.

Size is obviously one of the main differences between big and small cats. Another difference is the sounds that the two groups of cats can make. Small cats such as bobcats, lynx, and pet cats cannot roar, but they can purr continuously. Most big cats roar, but they cannot purr continuously. They can make a purring sound, but they have to stop to breathe in.

Leopard Country

The leopard is the world's most widespread cat, apart from the **domestic**, or pet, cat. Leopards live in most parts of Africa, south of the Sahara. They also live in the Middle East, across southern Asia, and down into Southeast Asia.

Leopards need only three things to survive: water to drink, animals to hunt and eat, and long grass or leafy cover so they can creep up on their **prey** unseen. Many different kinds of habitats provide the leopard with these basic necessities. Leopards are not that fussy about the types of animals they eat. They can, therefore, survive in forests, grasslands, dry areas, and high on mountains.

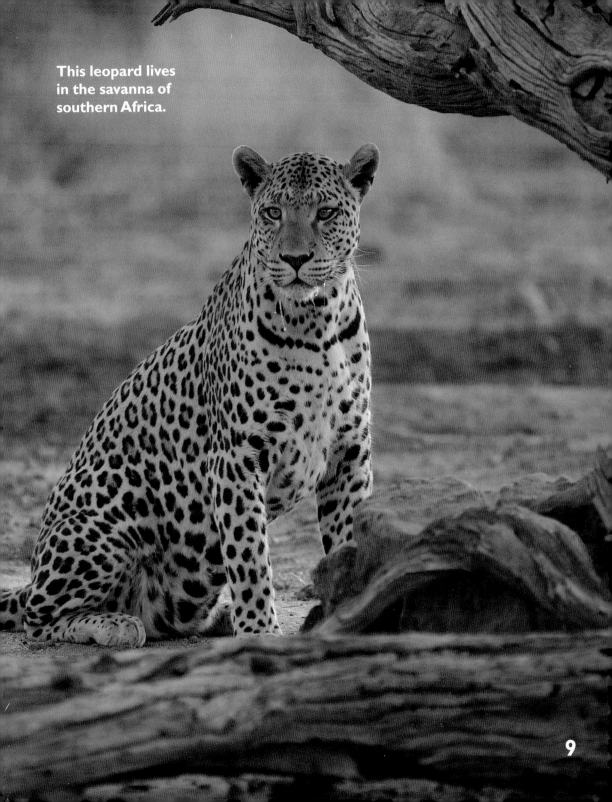

This leopard lives in the savanna of southern Africa.

With its large head, long body, and short legs, the leopard is compact, sturdy, and incredibly powerful.

Packed with Muscle

Adult leopards range from 3 to 7 feet (1 to 2 m) long. That is not counting the tail, which can add another 3 feet (1 m) to the animal's length! A big male can stand 30 inches (80 cm) tall and weigh nearly 200 pounds (90 kg). An adult female leopard is usually about half the weight of an adult male.

Leopards are not the largest members of the cat family. Lions and tigers can be more than twice their size. However, what a leopard lacks in size, it makes up for in power. These cats are packed with muscle, especially on their shoulders and **haunches**. That makes them speedy and also very strong.

Spotted Coat

Almost every inch of a leopard's body is patterned with dark markings. In fact, there are only a few places on a leopard that do not have spots, such as the eyes, ears, and nose. The background fur is tawny on the upper body, with paler fur on the belly, chest, and legs.

The markings on the the leopard's back and shoulders are arranged in patterns called **rosettes**. These markings almost look like a leopard's paw prints. There are smaller blotches and spots on the head, chest, and legs. Some leopards have markings that join up around the neck and look like a necklace.

Each leopard has a
unique pattern of
spots on its coat.

13

This leopard, hidden in the grass, lives in Sri Lanka, an island off India.

14

In Disguise

A leopard's spots don't just look beautiful—they are also very useful. They help the animal to blend in with its surroundings, whether it is hiding up a tree or crouched in the long grass. This natural disguise, called **camouflage**, is very important. It allows the leopard to sneak up on its prey without being seen.

The leopard's spotted fur is similar to that of its relative, the jaguar, which lives in South America. However, jaguars have dark spots in the center of each rosette. The leopard's rosettes have pale centers. Amazingly, no two leopards have exactly the same markings. Scientists studying these big cats in the wild can identify individual animals by their coat.

Black Panthers

Some leopards don't seem to have any spots at all. They are called black panthers. These big cats are not really black, but rather very dark brown. And they do have spots, but they can only be seen in bright sunlight because the rest of the fur is dark, too.

Black panthers are found mainly in the dense, dark forests of Southeast Asia. There, their dark color makes it easier for them to stalk prey through the shady forest. If a black panther **mates** with an ordinary tawny leopard, some of the young, or **cubs**, will probably be dark, too. If two black panthers mate, all of their **offspring** might be dark—just like the parents.

Black panthers rarely
survive on the plains of
Africa. Their dark coat
makes it difficult to blend
into the pale grass as
they stalk prey.

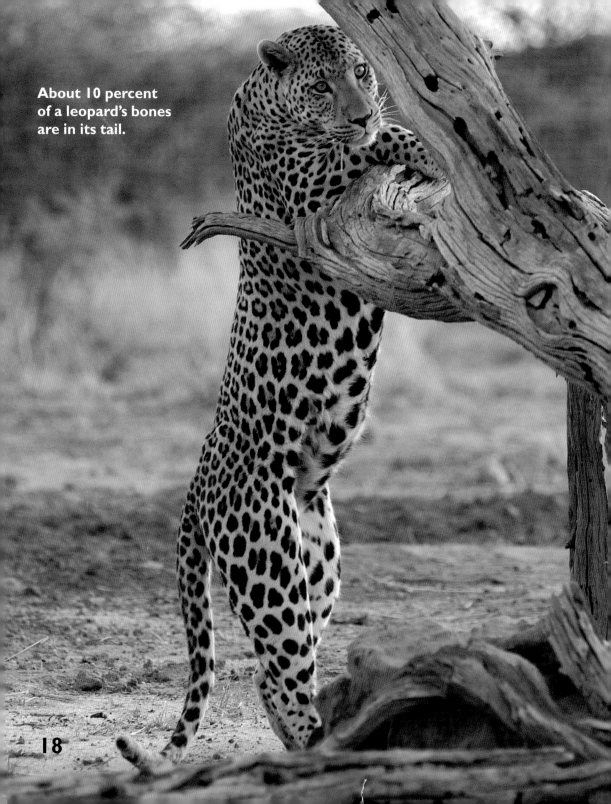

About 10 percent
of a leopard's bones
are in its tail.

Long, Swishy Tail

A leopard's tail can be almost as long as its body. Like the rest of the coat, the fur on the tail has dark spots and patches. The leopard can move its tail in various ways. For example, it can twitch the tip slightly or swish the whole tail from side to side.

The leopard's tail has many uses. It helps the animal balance as it runs, leaps, and climbs. Using its tail to balance, the leopard can walk along a narrow branch without slipping.

The underside of the tail is white. The female arches her tail over her back as she leads her cubs through dense vegetation. The pale tail works like a **beacon**, guiding the cubs as they move through the undergrowth.

Champion Athlete

Leopards are amazing athletes. They are very skilled at running, leaping, and swimming. They use these talents to catch their prey.

Leopards usually move quite slowly. But if they need to, they can race along at up to 40 miles (60 km) per hour. At that rate, they would break the speed limit on many roads! They are also strong swimmers and sometimes hunt water creatures.

Leopards are champion long jumpers. A leopard could leap a river 20 feet (6 m) wide without even getting its paws wet! That's like jumping the length of two family cars parked front to back. Leopards can also leap 10 feet (3 m) straight up in the air—as high as a basketball hoop!

Like most other cat species, the leopard is an expert tree climber.

Unlike humans, leopards have poor color vision. They mainly see the world in black and white and shades of gray.

Super Senses

Leopards hunt by day or night. They usually hunt at night in areas where humans live. That's because leopards prefer to avoid humans, who are more likely to be around during the day. A leopard's senses are fine-tuned, so it can find food as easily at night as it can by day.

A leopard has a keen sense of smell and sharp hearing. Its round ears swivel back and forth to pinpoint the origin of a sound. The leopard uses its long, sensitive whiskers on its snout to feel its way in the dark.

A leopard can see about as well as a human can by day. However, it can see much better in darkness than a person can. At the back of the inside of the leopard's eyes is a layer that reflects light. That allows the leopard to see well in dim light, such as starlight or moonlight. Night vision, keen smell, and super hearing help the hunter hone in on its prey.

What's for Dinner?

Like all cats, leopards are **carnivores**, or meat eaters. They don't care what's for dinner as long as it's meat! They will eat just about any animal they come across, from tiny beetles to massive wildebeest and young giraffes. The leopard's favorite prey are medium-sized animals, such as gazelles, pigs, and monkeys. Such animals provide a filling meal and do not struggle too much.

Small animals that leopards also hunt include frogs, rats, and birds. They are also fond of fish. Leopards often lie by rivers, hooking out fish with their claws. When all other food is scarce, leopards will eat eggs, fruit, and even grass. These unfussy feeding habits are the reason why leopards are able to live in so many places, from moist forests to dry scrublands.

Claws and Jaws

All hunting animals need weapons to catch and kill their prey. A leopard's weapons are similar to those of a domestic cat, but much more deadly! The massive paws are armed with curving claws that help the leopard to climb trees and also grip its prey. When not in use, the animal **retracts** its claws. That prevents the claws from becoming worn down and keeps them very sharp. When the leopard is ready to strike, it extends its claws.

Leopards have very powerful jaws that they use to clamp down on their victims. Four long fanglike teeth called **canines** seize the prey in a vicelike grip. Strong back teeth slice flesh into pieces that are small enough for the leopard to swallow. The leopard's tongue has tiny hooks that make it rough, much like sandpaper. The leopard uses its tongue to strip the skin off its prey and **rasp** every last bit of meat from its victims' bones.

Scientists divide leopards into seven different kinds, or subspecies, depending on where they live. This one is an African leopard, which is the most common of the subspecies.

Gone Hunting

A leopard usually hunts alone. As the animal moves stealthily through the undergrowth, its spotted coat makes it almost invisible. When it senses a possible victim, it freezes, crouches low, and then slithers closer. When it gets within pouncing range, it lunges forward, and springs on the animal's back to knock it off its feet. The leopard kills its prey with a bite to the back of the neck or by seizing its throat. The victim dies of **suffocation**. The leopard is so sneaky that its victims often die without ever knowing what it was that attacked them.

Leopards also ambush their prey from above. They lie along a low branch in a tree and drop onto any unsuspecting animal that wanders below. They also chase birds and monkeys through the treetops and sometimes hunt in water. In fact, nowhere is safe when there's a leopard on the prowl.

Forward-facing eyes allow a leopard to judge distances accurately as it prepares to pounce.

Leopards spend a lot of time in trees—eating, resting, avoiding enemies, or waiting to jump onto unsuspecting prey.

Save It for Later

When a leopard kills a big animal, such as a gazelle, it cannot eat all the meat at once. It feeds hungrily until its belly is full, but there's still a lot left. To keep its kill safe from **scavengers**, such jackals and hyenas, the leopard hides its kill up a tree.

The leopard uses its great strength to haul the prey—often weighing more than itself— up the tree. The cat heaves and strains with its powerful shoulders, until the prey is slung over a high branch. Now the leopard can feed in peace. It returns to its kill day after day, until every scrap of meat has been eaten.

Trespassers Beware!

Every leopard has its own private hunting ground. That is called its **territory**, or **home range**. The size of these territories varies. If food is plentiful, the patch can be small—as little as 4 square miles (10 sq km). If prey is scarce, the leopard needs a much bigger area to hunt in.

Female leopards do not mind other females in the neighborhood, and their home ranges often overlap. But a male will not put up with another male in his territory. He patrols the borders of his range, scratching trees and spraying these marks with his strongly scented urine. These scratch marks act as "keep out" signs, warning other leopards that this patch is taken. The territory holder will threaten and try to scare away male intruders. If neither animal retreats, the two will fight.

A leopard makes
scratch marks on
a tree trunk. Its sharp
claws are made of
a tough substance
called keratin.

The white dot of fur on the back of this leopard's right ear can be clearly seen. Some scientists think that the dots might look like eyes to other animals.

Dotty Ears

On the back of each of their cup-shaped ears, leopards have a white patch of fur, surrounded by dark fur. Scientists believe these dots help cubs follow their mother through dense forest. The clearly visible marks make it easier for the youngsters to keep track of their mother.

So why do male leopards have the marks, too? They don't need to have them to guide cubs, because they hardly ever help raise their young. Some scientists think leopards use their ear spots to signal to other leopards, on the rare occasions when they meet up to mate or hunt. With one flick of its ear, a leopard can send all sorts of signals, such as "come closer," "the prey went that way," or "go away!"

Leopard Noises

Leopards are not known as noisy animals. But they can produce various sounds to communicate with other leopards if they want to. Like other big cats, leopards can roar. However, a leopard's roar sounds more like a rasping cough than a lion's full-throated roar. Male leopards warn other males away by roaring. Female leopards produce a quiet roar when they are ready to mate. Leopards can also grunt and purr.

Scientists who study leopards in the wild have heard leopards make two other noises. One is a **chuffling** sound, which the animal produces by blowing through its nose. The other is a high-pitched chirp. Female leopards make both of these sounds to call their cubs or to warn them that an enemy is approaching.

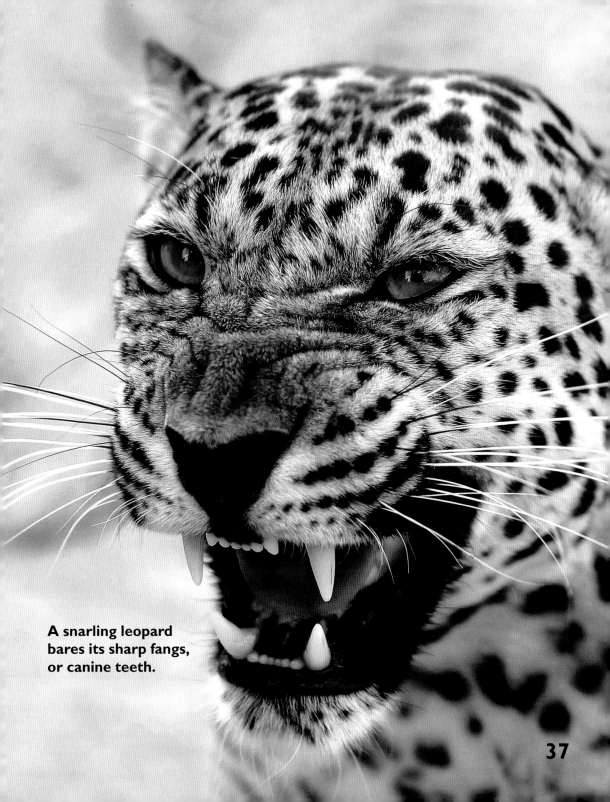

A snarling leopard
bares its sharp fangs,
or canine teeth.

Male and female leopards spend little time together. After they have mated, the female usually chases away the male.

Two's Company

Leopards are mainly solitary animals. When a male and female come together to mate, they spend only a few days together. Then they go their separate ways again. The female almost always raises her cubs alone, though scientists do know of a few occasions when the father has helped rear the young.

Many animals mate and have their young at a particular time of year. In contrast, leopard cubs can be born in any season. When a female is ready to mate, she wanders around. She leaves scent markings and quietly roars. These signs tell the males she is ready to mate.

Welcome, Cubs!

Between three and four months after mating, the female prepares to give birth. She seeks out a den such as a cave or a clump of trees. There the cubs will spend their first weeks, hidden from enemies such as hyenas.

Leopards give birth to between one and six cubs at a time. The group of young is called a **litter**. Most litters contain two or three cubs.

Newborn leopards weigh about one pound (450 g). The cubs are covered with gray fur with just a hint of the spotted markings. With eyes tightly closed, the youngsters are helpless. They spend their time snuggling in a furry bundle with their brothers and sisters. They wriggle over one another to reach their mother's rich milk.

A leopard mother is very
protective of her young.
Lions, hyenas, and other
leopards will kill leopard
cubs if given the chance.

A cub knows
to keep still and
quiet when its
mother carries
it to a new den.

First Steps

After about a week, a baby leopard's eyes open. It takes its first wobbly steps at about two weeks old. But the cub stays firmly put in the den when its mother goes out hunting—even if she is gone for a long time and it gets hungry.

Female leopards are fiercely protective of their cubs. Every few days, the mother might move her youngsters to a new hiding place just to keep them safe from **predators**. She moves her cubs one at a time by lifting each one by the scruff of the neck. The baby becomes limp until it is set back on the ground.

The female is an affectionate mother. She spends a lot of time washing her youngsters. When she comes back after hunting, family members greet one another by rubbing faces.

Play with a Purpose

The cubs have a lot to learn before they can take their place as adult leopards. At six to eight weeks, they leave the den and get their first look at the big, wide world. On their first trip, they go only a short way before crouching in the shadows. As they get stronger, they venture farther from the den.

The cubs will now get their first lessons in the tricky art of hunting. Their first target is their mother's tail! As the mother twitches her tail back and forth, the young chase after it. They try to pounce on it with their small paws. They also play-fight with one another.

Before long, the cubs are chasing after real prey such as crickets and lizards. At last, the big day comes, and the cub makes its first kill.

Play-fighting teaches cubs how to wrestle another animal to the ground—an important lesson for when they will have to hunt to survive.

A wide-eyed cub spots some prey and begins to plan its attack, under the supervision of its mother.

Learning to Hunt

At four to six months old, the cubs start to go out with their mother on hunting trips. The young leopards learn by watching their mother as she stalks, catches, and kills prey. The mother lets her young try, too, keeping a careful watch.

Hunting lessons can be dangerous. Cubs can get badly injured or even killed when fierce prey, such as baboons and pigs, fight back with teeth, claws, and hooves. Gradually, the cubs get more experienced, and by about 18 months old they are able to hunt on their own.

Time to Go

At about one year old, the cub has learned most of what it needs to know to be an adult leopard. Most cubs stick close to their mother for at least a year. Some cubs stay nearly two years, but eventually the mother is ready to give birth again. That is the signal that it's time for the cubs to leave.

Young female leopards might be allowed to take over part of their mother's range. Young males must go farther away and set up their own territories. At the age of three years, leopards start to breed. With luck, and if they have learned their lessons well, they could live for more than ten years and have many cubs of their own.

Words to Know

Beacon   A light or something bright, serving as a guide to follow.

Camouflage   The colors and patterns on an animal's skin or fur that help it to blend in with its surroundings.

Canines   Long, sharp teeth used to grab prey.

Carnivores   Animals that feed mainly on meat.

Chuffling   A sound made when leopards breathe out sharply through their nostrils.

Cubs   Young leopards.

Domestic   Tamed or bred by humans.

Haunches   Hindquarters or hips of an animal.

Home range   The area in which an animal lives and searches for food.

Litter   A group of young animals.

Mates   Comes together to produce young.

Offspring   The young of animals.

Predators   Animals that hunt other animals.

Prey   An animal that is hunted by another animal for food.

Rasp   To rub with something rough.

Retracts   Draws back inside the body.

Rosettes   Circular markings made up of spots.

Scavengers   Animals such as hyenas that steal other animals' kills.

Suffocation   When an animal cannot breathe.

Territory   An area that an animal defends as its own personal space.

Find Out More

Books

Feeny, K. *Leopards*. Our Wild World. Minnetonka, Minnesota: NorthWord Books for Young Readers, 2002.

Squire, A. O. *Leopards*. True Books: Animals. Danbury, Connecticut: Children's Press, 2005.

Web sites

Leopard
www.enchantedlearning.com/subjects/mammals/cats/leopard/
Leopardprintout.shtml
A printout and facts about leopards.

Leopard (Panthera pardus)
animals.nationalgeographic.com/animals/mammals/
leopard.html
A profile of the leopard.

Index

A, B, C
ambushing 28
belly 12, 28, 31
big cats 5, 7, 36
birth 40, 48
biting 28, 32
black panthers 16, 17
body 10
bones 18
camouflage 15
canine teeth 25, 37
carnivores 24
cat family 5
chest 12
chuffling 36
claws 24, 25, 33
climbing 19, 21, 25
clouded leopards 7
coat 5, 12, 13, 15, 17,
    19, 28
communication 36
cubs 16, 19, 35, 39, 40, 41,
    42, 42, 43, 44, 46, 47, 48

D, E, F
den 40, 43, 44
domestic cats 5, 8, 25
ears 23, 34, 35

eyes 23, 29, 40
fighting 32
fur 12, 15, 16, 19, 34,
    35, 40

H, J
habitats 8, 24
hearing 23
height 11
home range 32, 48
hunting 5, 8, 20, 23, 25, 28,
    32, 35, 43, 44, 45, 47
jaguars 7, 15
jaws 25

K, L, M
keratin 33
leaping 19, 20
legs 10, 12
length 11
life span 48
lions 7, 11, 36, 41
litter 40
mating 16, 35, 36, 38, 39, 40

N, P, R
neck 12, 40, 43
nose 36

paws 25, 44
play-fighting 44, 45
predators 43
prey 8, 15, 16, 17, 20,
    23, 24, 25, 28, 31,
    44, 46, 47
purring 7, 36
roaring 7, 36
rosettes 12, 15
running 19, 20

S, T, V, W
scavengers 31
scent 32, 39
scratch marks 32, 33
small cats 7
smell 23
snow leopard 6, 7
subspecies 26
swimming 20
tail 11, 18, 19, 44
teeth 25
territory 32, 48
tigers 7, 11
tongue 25
vision 22, 23
weight 11, 40
whiskers 23